EASY SONGWRITING FOR THE BEGINNER

4 Steps to Your First Song

Copyright @ Solomon Igboayaka 2020

The right of the author has been asserted by him in accordance with the copy right writing, designs and patent act of the United Kingdom.

A catalogue copy of this book is available in the British Library.

All rights reserved. No part of this book may be reproduced, stored or transmitted by any means whether auditory, graphic, mechanical, or electronic without the written permission of the author, except in the case of brief excerpts used in critical articles and reviews. Unauthorised reproduction of any part of this work is illegal and is punishable by law.

Unless otherwise noted, the author and the publisher make no explicit guarantees as the accuracy of the information contained in this book may differ based on individual experiences and context.

REVIEWS

"This is a simple, well written book that has done what it says on the cover. Easy Song Writing is a resource that is most needed in times like this when most people need to connect with their innermost self. I believe that as the reader uses the easy to follow steps in the book, a deep sense of satisfaction and pride will be experienced. This is a must-read for anyone who wants to experience in full the ingrained nature that God has given everyone."

Dr. Chris Gbenle

Senior Pastor, Fountain of Love RCCG Scotland

"This book acutely unpacks a very interesting topic in an engaging, concise and practical manner, which is a rare combination these days. I particularly enjoyed the presentation and could clearly identify with the passion of the writer as it filtered through gently but convincingly. The writer addressed some age-long myths about song writing and carefully demystifies some of these concepts with an aim to put them in their right perspectives.

With every word in this book, I could see a true worshipper's heart for something new, fresh and personal in the desire to prepare a delicacy for the King of kings through songs. This is a great read and would recommend for everyone, especially those who would want to express their love to God (or even their loved ones) through songs".

Dr. David Emele

Singer, song writer, worship leader and Director of Music,

RCCG Scotland

"This book brought back memories of when I started writing songs as an 8 year old. Its *simple exposition gently guides you through easy steps to song writing. You may find yourself itching to write a song from Chapter 1".*

David D'Amadeus Ayeni

"Thank you for debunking the myth that you need a special talent to be a songwriter in your book. Anybody can write a song, you just need to believe in yourself. I believe this book will break some preconceived notions and set people free to write their songs and if for nothing just to leave a legacy and bless someone".

"And Oh yea Grammy here we come".

Eloho Efemuai

JUST TO SAY THANK YOU FOR BUYING THIS BOOK, I'M OFFERING YOU A FREE GIFT.

1) BOOK A FREE SESSION WITH THE AUTHOR TO WORK ON YOUR SONG!

CLICK LINK BELOW

https://mailchi.mp/0a901391e1c9/book-a-free-session

2) DOWNLOAD A FREE COPY OF THE WORLD CLASS SINGLES "REMEMBER" OR "MOST HIGH"!

CLICK LINK BELOW

https://mailchi.mp/ba170d62e0f9/download-a-free-single

TABLE OF CONTENTS

CHAPTER 1 9

INTRODUCTION 9

1.1 BREAKING MINDSET BLOCKS OR PARADIGMS 12

1.2 WHY SHOULD I BOTHER? WHY SHOULD I WRITE A SONG? OF WHAT BENEFIT IS IT? WHYYYYYYY? 17

CHAPTER 2 20

LET'S GET STARTED 20

2.1 SO WHAT IS A SONG? 22

2.2 WHAT ARE LYRICS? 24

2.3 SONG STRUCTURE 25

CHAPTER 3 27

THE SONGWRITING PROCESS 27

3.1 HOW TO GET INSPIRATION 29

3.2 RECORD YOUR IDEAS 39

CHAPTER 4 41

4 STEPS 41

LAST WORDS FROM ME..................................50

CHAPTER 1

INTRODUCTION

The principles and process of song writing are universal in the world of music. The same ingredients are required to put a song together and it doesn't matter whether it's a secular song or a gospel song. What does matter, is that the end product of a finished song is achieved. This book however addresses song writing from the perspective of a Christian.

Whenever the topic of Song-writing comes up, a lot of people think it is or try to make it out to be something very complex. I am here to break it down and make it an easy and fun activity that every Christian can engage in, to whatever degree he or she wants.

So many Christians love the idea of worshipping God with a song. Some would like to write and sing the songs being birthed in their hearts to the Lord. However, a large proportion lack the confidence to do so, some lack a supportive environment that encourages their creativity, some believe it is too difficult etc. After 26 years of writing all kinds of gospel-centric songs, I believe this is one area that I can help others in developing their innate skill.

Before we go any further, I would like to clarify the objective of this book so that we do not have unrealistic expectations. This book is meant to help you START writing your own songs. It is NOT designed or intended to turn you into a Grammy or Dove award winning songwriter. If that happens, well and good. However the primary aim is to move you from the position of just wishing to write, or thinking it is impossible, to writing your first song. If at the end of reading this book you write your first song, then I have accomplished my objective of helping you birth the songs that have been lying fallow within you. Once the first song is done, it becomes easier to write the next and the next and like any skill in life, you will become better and better in your compositions as you keep on writing.

1.1 BREAKING MINDSET BLOCKS OR PARADIGMS

The first thing I'm going to say here is that ANYBODY can write a song. That's right you heard me correctly. ANYBODY can write a song. You don't have to be a musician. You don't have to be able to read staff/stave music or understand tonic solfa notations. As long as you can hum a melody, you can write a song.

Now whether it's a good song or not is an entirely different matter. You also do not have to be a superstar or megastar, you don't have to be a recording artiste, release an album or single or be "called" into music ministry to write a song. All you need is a desire and an interest.

Hmmm....... I just used a couple of terms that you may or may not know the meaning of. So let me explain.

Tonic Solfa: Do you remember the classic movie "Sound of Music"? When Maria was teaching the von Trapp children how to sing she said "do - a deer a female deer, re - a drop of golden sun, mi - a name I call myself, fa - a longer way to run, so - I need a pulley train, la - a note to follow so, ti - I drink with jam and bread, that will bring us back to do, do, do, do". Simply put, **do re mi fa so la ti do** are syllables that represent the relationship between the tones of a key. Your Dictionary online defines it as "*a system of musical notation based on the relationship between the tones of a key, using the syllables of solmization (do, re, mi, etc.) instead of the usual staff symbols: used in teaching singing*".

Staff/Stave Music: Otherwise known as sheet music. When you watch all these classical orchestras, you will notice that each musician/instrument has a sheet of paper in front of them from which they play. This sheet of music is covered with symbols and lines. Therefore, the Encyclopaedia Brittanica defines it thus: "***Staff**, also*

spelled **stave**, in the notation of Western music, five parallel horizontal lines that, with a clef, indicate the pitch of musical notes".
Below is an example:

Some people say or think "but I'm not a singer" or "I'm not good enough" or "It's only meant for special people" or "I can't play an instrument" or "I don't know where to start" or "I don't know what genre or style". All these 'obstacles' are completely irrelevant to song writing. There are only 2

fundamental things required to put a song together:

1) A melody i.e the tune

2) The lyrics i.e the words that make up the song

Every other thing like the instrument music, part harmonies, backing vocals etc are all what I would call "accessories" to the song. Let me use an analogy that everyone should be able to relate to. If you think of a black dress (evening gown) as the melody and lyrics, then the necklace, earrings, brooch, bracelet, shoes etc are the music, backing vocals and part harmonies.

1.2 WHY SHOULD I BOTHER? WHY SHOULD I WRITE A SONG? OF WHAT BENEFIT IS IT? WHYYYYYYY?

This is a very valid question and answering it will provide the internal motivation to not just start to write these songs but also to complete the process.

- To express in your own words, way and style your adoration, love for, and worship of your God
- To birth the music that has been in your heart and spirit and make it tangible
- To be fruitful and original - You are an original creation of God. There is only one you and no-one can

be you as well as you. Therefore everything that comes out of you based on the gifts/talents you have been endued with, is an original piece and a fruit from that seed.

- To bless someone else
- To leave a legacy for generations to come
- To "trade" with the talent/ gift God has given you (like the parable of the talents)
- To discover your own hidden depths
- To generate a revenue stream eventually (you never can tell which of your songs will gain traction globally)
- To die empty

CHAPTER 2

LET'S GET STARTED

As I said previously, the two fundamental ingredients for a song are a melody or tune and lyrics or words.

Some people get a melody first and then start to put words together to match that melody. Some others have words first and then start to look for a melody that will match those words. There is no hard and fast rule to it. Whichever one comes to you first, flow with it and work from there. Some people find that they can write poetry but don't know how to translate that into a tune. Not to worry help is at hand. Something, I believe I should address at this point is the misconception that you have to write a song from beginning to end by yourself. That is not true. You can get help from your friends or other musical people around you. A song can be a collaborative affair or team effort. It is possible that you write a chorus but have no ideas for the verse. Don't feel shy to ask for help from someone you believe can help you.

It is also possible that the entire song is just a chorus. By that I mean there are no verses, bridges, refrains or vamps.

2.1 SO WHAT IS A SONG?

The Cambridge English Dictionary defines it as "a usually short piece of music with words that are sung".

"At its most basic, a **song** is a short piece of music, usually with words. It combines melody and vocals, although some composers have written **instrumental pieces**, or musical works without words, that mimic the quality of a singing voice. The words of a song are called **lyrics**. Lyrics can include a series of **verses**, the longer sections of the song that tell the story, and a **refrain**, a short phrase repeated at the end of every verse. Songs can have a simple structure of one or two verses, or a more complex one with multiple verses and refrains.

Songs usually have a **meter** or beat. Whether you sing or speak the lyrics, you can feel a pattern or pulse in the way the words move the song forward.

The word 'song' has been around for a very long time, and it connects back to Old English and Old Norse languages. This history suggests that songs are used for many purposes: to tell stories, express emotions, or convey a belief in faith. Sometimes they give instructions or help make difficult, repetitive work a little less tiresome".

2.2 WHAT ARE LYRICS?

Lyrics are the words that ride on the melody of the song. They are the words used to express the ebbs and flows of the melody. They are the words used to communicate the theme of the song to the listener.

Now, the lyrics of every song will have an over-arching theme. This theme (most of the time) will be embedded or encapsulated in the chorus. The verse(s), will serve the purpose of expounding on that theme i.e going into more detail or explanation. Your next question might be "How do I decide on a theme?" Thankfully, as Christians the Bible is a one-stop shop for not just themes but also the lyrics required to express those themes. For instance, you just repented of a conscious sin you committed and you're remorseful and contrite so you want to sing about God's mercy/forgiveness and restoration. The book of Psalms provides a lot of material to draw from/ draw on. Or you want to sing/write about God's majesty and glory? The books of Isaiah and Revelations provide material for that. Or you want to sing or write about Jesus' love and nature and miracles? The books of Matthew, Mark, Luke and John provide that.

2.3 SONG STRUCTURE

In talking about song structure, my intention here is not to delve too deeply into the details and technicalities but rather give you an idea or overview of the different traditional structures that most (if not all) successful songs fall into.

These are inclusive of but not limited to the following:

Chorus

Chorus-Verse-Chorus

Verse-Chorus

Verse-Chorus -Verse-Chorus

Verse-Chorus-Verse-Chorus-Bridge-Chorus

CHAPTER 3

THE SONGWRITING PROCESS

In this chapter we will be going through the whole song writing process. Where do you start from? How do you go about it? What pointers do I have that will make the process easier and quicker? I'll be addressing all these questions and more as we go along. Rest assured, you're not alone on this journey so get ready to have some fun while we make some music together. (This is where I would normally have included a smiley face.)

Okay, enough of that! Let's move on!

The first thing that is required in the song writing process is inspiration. Oh yes! Without inspiration we would never have heard any of the works of Mozart, Beethoven, Wagner (pronounced VAGNER), Tchaikovsky, Bach or Handel, Brooklyn Tabernacle Choir, Michael Jackson, Cece Winans, Phil Thompson, Shaggy, Hillsong, Fred Hammond etc. You noticed of course that I listed both secular and Christian musicians didn't you? This is because inspiration is a requirement to produce ANY kind of music or write ANY song.

3.1 HOW TO GET INSPIRATION

There are quite a number of ways in which inspiration for songs can be obtained. Some of them include:

Life Experiences: Various occurrences in our lives can provide the inspiration for a song. It could be the birth of a child and the circumstances surrounding it, it could be the death of a loved one, it could be success in a particular endeavour, it could be heartbreak from a love relationship etc. Whatever the event may be, inspiration can be drawn from it to write a song. I'll give you a couple of examples. You know the popular hymn "It is well" (written by Horatio

Spafford) that starts "When peace like a river attendeth my way.."?

Are you aware that this song was written after a series of tragic events had occurred in his life? His 4 year old son had died then his properties were engulfed in the Chicago Fire of 1871 and finally his 4 daughters died at sea. It was only his wife that survived the sea collision. It was on his way to meet his grieving wife that he penned "It is well" which has been and still is a blessing to the Church for hundreds of years. I'll give you another example and this one is personal. In 1995 or 1996 I was travelling by bus in Nigeria between Owerri and Onitsha when we ran into armed robbers that had set up a road block. We had just been overtaken by a saloon car when all of sudden we saw his brake lights come on hard and heard gun shots in the air. The driver immediately parked the car and we all struggled to get out of the bus (knocking out the sliding door in the process). We then ran up the hill into the bush and farmland accompanied by the sound of gunshots and semi-automatic firing. Now, I was carrying a travelling bag strapped to my back that was filled with cash so while scrabbling to climb up the hill, the weight of the bag kept dragging me down.

I eventually got to the top and ran into the bush where we all waited until the sound of gunfire subsided and the robbers left. Once we got back into the bus to continue our journey, I was inspired to write a song with the following lyrics for the chorus and second verse:

Chorus:

Your Name is Jesus Shepherd of my soul

Suddenly out of confusion You rescue me whole

Constantly protecting me and I don't know what to say

But You alone O Lord are worthy of my praise today

Verse 2:

When the going gets rough and situations get tough

You are always there to lift me up and keep me safe from harm

You rescue me deliver me and put my feet on solid ground

Now I can sing to You because You've kept me safe and sound

Scriptures : Another avenue to get inspiration for song writing is through the Word of God aka the Holy Bible. This could happen during the Word session of a church service or during your own personal Bible study time. I was in a Wednesday service (which is our midweek Bible Study) when I was inspired to write "I Surrender To Your Will" which is a simple chorus

I surrender to Your will

All my heart my mind my will

Lord I surrender, I surrender, I surrender

To Your will

Donnie McClurkin has said over and over again that he was inspired to write the song "Only You Are Holy" while he was in service and we all know how much impact that song has had on the Body of Christ.

Now you can also be inspired while studying the Word on your own. Maranatha Singers took Psalm 25:1-2 and made it a beautiful song that has blessed so many over the ages. The lyrics are:

Unto Thee O Lord

Do I lift up my soul

O My God I trust in Thee

Let me not be afraid

Let not my enemy triumph over me

Personal worship or quiet time: During your quiet time or personal private worship sessions, you can be inspired with new songs. Sometimes you remember these songs long after your worship session is over and some other times you completely forget them. I have personally written most of my songs while having my quiet time or just enjoying worshipping God. I remember the first Christian song I wrote was one week after re-dedicating my life to Jesus in June of 1994. The chorus went thus:

I will worship You Lord in everything I say and do

I will worship You Lord 'cos Jesus You have been so true

In everything I do Lord

I will worship You

Listening to the kind of music you want to write: There is a saying, "You are what you eat" and this is very true when it comes to song writing. The kind of music you listen to (consume), determines the kind of songs you end up writing. There's a secular artiste I love called Shaggy. I used to listen to him steadily when I was in university. I used to sing his songs and mimic him since I love reggae and dancehall. It was such that even when I wrote my own reggae songs that required a patois section, I would deliver it with my "Shaggy" flavour. Fast forward 14 years after leaving university, anyone that listened to my world class single "Remember" that was released in 2016 would comment that I sound like Shaggy. Having said that, I have also intentionally spent time listening to other genres that I wanted to write like e.g Bethel Music and Elevation and I have succeeded in writing similar songs.

At this point I must state that I am a firm believer in getting the Holy Spirit involved in your song writing because He is the one that inspires us, leads us into all truth, reveals the hidden things to us, and teaches us how to get into the city. Therefore I encourage you to:

1) Ask for His help to write a song

2) Spend time in worship

3) Spend time meditating on the Word

4) Listen to the kind of music you would like to write i.e singers and songs that inspire you

5) Be observant of or Pay attention to the things going on around you e.g nature, politics, world events, events in your personal life and career etc

These are just some of the sources from which inspiration for song writing comes.

3.2 RECORD YOUR IDEAS

Sometimes you may receive or get a really good melody or set of lyrics and then forget what that tune was a few minutes later. That can be very frustrating so please, please use your phone and record the ideas you get so you can revisit them later.

I have so many different voice notes recorded on my phones and tablet and these help me when I want to continue working on any song. Of course, some of them end up being discarded but at least I have a record of them for use potentially.

CHAPTER 4

4 STEPS

In this chapter, I have outlined the 4 steps required to write any song. They are:

1. Choose or Decide on a theme or concept you want to sing about
2. Get a tune or melody
3. Pen lyrics for verse or chorus
4. Choose song title

Steps 2 & 3 do not necessarily have to be in that order. Since this is a creative art, you could have step 3 before step 2. However, these 4 steps are indispensable to successfully writing any song.

So let's break it down.

1. Choose or Decide On A Theme Or Concept You Want To Sing About

Every song has an over arching theme or concept but deciding on what that theme will be is sometimes a bit difficult. This is because there are so many themes to write on. For example love, mercy, forgiveness, vengeance, deliverance, protection, healing, betrayal, restoration, faith, joy, victory, success, anger, hurt and pain, unforgiveness, bitterness, heart ache, death of a loved one, sickness, miracles, romance, family breakdown, politics, prophecy, global events, pandemics or plagues, faithfulness, repentance, generosity or giving, etc.

As you can see, it can be a bit daunting with so many options. However once this part is decided, you can then move on to the next steps of finding a melody and lyrics.

On the other hand, the theme could also be informed by inspiration. By this I mean you may already be inspired with a melody and lyrics. You may have actually finished the writing process before you realise that the theme is one thing or another.

2. Getting A Tune or Melody

Achieving this can be through different means. It can be done mechanically by just humming tunes and playing with them i.e trial and error or by pure inspiration from the Holy Spirit. Remember God is a Spirit and they that worship Him must worship Him in spirit and in truth (John 4:24). Remember also that ALL music originated from God. He is the Source of ALL things. There are a number of platforms online where you can obtain fully completed songs without lyrics. Some producers put fully mastered work online for free and all you need to do is just generate your own lyrics that will match the melodies and music. You could also get/develop a melody by listening to certain chords or progressions being played on an instrument e.g the keyboard or guitar or maybe even a saxophone.

3. Pen Lyrics For Verse Or Chorus

Putting lyrics together for the verse or chorus is usually the toughest part (in my opinion). Some people are prolific wordsmiths and some others, not so much.

The objective here is to use words to express the chosen theme within the confines of the melody. There should be words that rhyme and as such provide a poetic flow and rhythm. I should say here that something you need to take into consideration is the fact that as the years go by, the style of lyrical expression changes. I mean the way lyrics were used to express different concepts and feelings in the past has changed. For instance, the way romance was expressed in song in the 1970s is very different from how it was expressed in the 2000s. I'm just saying that you need to use the right words in your day that will maximally communicate the ideas and feelings you want to convey in your song.

4. Choose A Song Title

Take a breath! At this point you can pat yourself on the back! You have succeeded in choosing a theme to write/sing about, you've succeeded in getting a melody/tune for the song, you have succeeded in actually writing lyrics for the chorus and/or the remaining body of the song. So celebrate these milestones!!

Okay enough with the celebration!

Let's complete it with a nice bow on top by choosing a song title. Choosing a title sometimes is very straightforward but at other times it can be a bit tricky. The main thing to note here is that the title of your song traditionally would be found embedded in your chorus or verse (mostly in your chorus). It's usually a word or phrase that captures the essence of the theme and has been repeated over and over again in the song.

Sometimes because of the theme you've chosen to write about, you may have already chosen a song title. However, once the song is completed, you may find that your initial title doesn't quite carry the same punch any more. I mean it may not truly represent/ capture the essence of the song. I remember one of my songs that I was writing and the theme was on God's sovereignty so I had titled it "Sovereign". By the time I had finished writing and listened to it over and over again, I had to change the title to "Awesome God". There was another one that I had completed and titled "He Rules" but that had to be changed to "God In The Heavens".

Be that as it may, whatever the title you have chosen, you can now sit back, pour yourself a drink and savour the moment because you deserve it. You have now completed your first song. Well done!!

LAST WORDS FROM ME

If you enjoyed this book and found it helpful, feel free to share it with other people. I would also like to hear how you're getting on with your song writing. So feel free to drop me a line at strictlyjesus@gmail.com or you can follow me on my artiste page Solomon on Facebook. You'll find my social media handles below.

Guess what? I also have the Song Writing Hub on Youtube where we share tips on song writing. I would love to have you join us by subscribing to the channel. You might even get featured with your song there. Wouldn't that be ace?

#solomonsaysso

@solomonsaysso

@solomonsaysso

solomonsaysso

ACKNOWLEDGEMENTS

First and foremost, I would like to acknowledge my God and Maker, the One who has kept me all these years and made it possible for me to use and share the gift He has given me with the world. I love You Lord!

Next, I would like to acknowledge my wife Florence who has been a consistent support and motivator on this journey. I remember when she asked me if I was actually writing a book or blog because I'd written 1,500 words and declared I was done. Thanks so much for "cracking the whip" my darling. This book is the first fruit and testimonial to "Write That Book Already!"

Not to be forgotten are my wonderful siblings and editorial board: Kenneth, Anita and Eunice that provided feedback on the written work. Thanks so much for your input.

Finally, my review/launch team David Ayeni, David Emele, Alberta Karim, Alison Cran, Ogaga Esharefasa, Fola Sanwoolu, Imoh Ejumotan, Jacob Oapata, Emmanuel Nfor, Ify Odugbemi, Dotimi Egbuson, Grace Agbana, Deji Ade-Aina and Eloho Efemuai. You guys are the best.

www.ingramcontent.com/pod-product-compliance
Lightning Source LLC
Chambersburg PA
CBHW060858050426
42453CB00008B/1018